Sam's Dog

words by Josephine Croser
illustrated by Annie White

Sam has a dog.

They play.

"Go," said Sam.

The dog went.

"Come," said Sam.

The dog came.

"Up," said Sam.

The dog jumped up.

"Down," said Sam.

The dog jumped down.

A cat came.

The cat saw the dog.

The dog saw the cat.

"Come," said Sam.

But the dog went.